"I could identify with everything you said. Only after my husband read it could he finally understand what I was going through. Thanks, Sue for putting it into words."

– Cancer patient, Rancho Mirage, CA

"I drank in your words and felt your fears, your anguish, and your acceptance as you "moved on" through your ordeal with cancer. These are needed words, put so well to rhyme for those who are finding themselves taking your journey."

– Nancy Knowlton, Vail, Colorado

"I thought I would read one poem a night, but no, I gobbled it up! There were so many tender, sensitive, insightful images. Even though I have not had cancer, some of it could be related to other issues and so it spoke to my heart."

– Samantha Landy, Author and Speaker

"From all of us in this office and those who will be touched by your wisdom - thank you! Your book will be in the waiting room for all to read and gain strength and inspiration."

– Suzanne Campanile, Mammogram Technologist
Northern California Women's Imagining Center
Palo Alto, CA

"I never knew what the blue dots were or noticed them before. Thank you for this information. I can now be more sensitive to my patients who wear these blue dots."

– Doctor, Santa Clara, CA

Other Books by Sue McCollum

BRAVE and FREE

Real Love Stories Have No Endings...

Who Holds the Key?

Moving On
(before and after cancer)

Copyright @ 2002
by
Sue McCollum

First Edition - April 2002
Second Edition, revised - August 2002
Third Edition, revised - November 2004
Fourth Edition, revised - September 2005

All rights reserved. No part of this book may be reproduced in any other form without written permission from the publisher, except for review purposes.

ISBN 0-9722313-0-7

Published by
Blue Dot Publishing
P.O. Box 60725
Palo Alto, CA 94306

Printed by
Prodigy Press, Inc.
Palo Alto, CA

I Will Survive!

Life can change, at the turn of a screw,
When the word 'cancer' is spoken to you.
You're upset, you're frightened;
You don't know what to do.

I know I must own it,
and conquer it I will.
But in the present moment
I'm sick, tired, and ill.

Cancer and death, for many years,
have always been linked together.
I must change my mind and know today
that truth is not forever.

"I will survive, I'm not a victim!"
I will shout out each day.
Then I'll go home, fall on my knees,
and pray, and pray, and pray.

Moving On

Table of Contents

Dedication 9

Introduction 11

The Discovery

    The Little Pea 15

    "c" 17

    One in Three 19

    Choices 21

    Where Few Go 23

The Treatments

    Young and Male 27

    Blue Dots 29

    High Heels and a White Coat 31

    Radiation 33

    Clones 35

    Others 37

    Human Touch 39

The Follow up

    A Doctors' Knowledge 43

    First Checkup 45

    The Mammogram 47

    My Oncologist 49

    I'm All Yours 51

Life Goes On

   A Pretty Face..55

   Cocktail Party...57

   Victims - No More! 59

   Beautiful Smile...61

   Waiting in the Wings..63

   I've Learned 65

Dedication

This book is dedicated to all those who wear the blue dots*
Proud members of the Blue Dot Society.

Blue Dot Society

The Blue Dot Society is a special group
of strong and hearty folks.
They've stepped up to take their turn
to be pushed, prodded, and poked.

Their bodies perhaps a bit broken,
but their spirits are strong indeed;
To manage to go through what they must do
to finish this medical deed.

It takes hours to get these blue dots.
The technicians must be precise.
To place the dots just where they are
is not just a roll of the dice.

After they're placed and the treatments are finished,
you acknowledge what you've been through.
A very tough time, in your book of life,
but it's made you a stronger you.

So, be proud of your blue dots - don't cover them up.
Perhaps they do hold the answer.
To rid yourself of that horrid disease
the one they do call cancer.

* (Before treatment, the area to be radiated is first
tattooed with blue dots.)

Moving On

Introduction

In June of 1999 I heard those dreaded words, "Yes, Sue, it is cancer." As a writer, I have recorded this journey and share these pages with you.

It is a lonesome journey and I will be forever grateful for so many who supported me during this difficult time. I thank you from the bottom of my heart. I needed a God with skin and each of you provided that for me.

I would also like to thank my husband, Bob, who provided the strength for me when I had none and to my sons, Mike and Jeff, for walking this very lonesome and challenging walk with me.

Difficult times do make us stronger and we have all learned many valuable lessons from this experience.

My thanks also to those who encouraged me to write this book and to get it published.

My wish is that this book will speak to your heart and bless your life.

The Discovery

Moving On

The Little Pea

It had been a year since I found it.
It was like a little pea.
It didn't go away
so I went to the Doctor to see.

I didn't want to see the Doc.,
but I stepped up to the plate.
When the Doctor said, "It's cancer!"
I knew I couldn't wait.

Two surgeries, radiation,
and six months of chemo too.
By the time they got finished with me,
I didn't know what to do.

I thought of this as an 'ugly job.'
It has a start and finish.
I will not let cancer own me
nor my life will it diminish.

I'll continue to hike and to walk,
I will enjoy each minute.
With my family and my dear friends
I will, indeed, win it.

Moving On

'c' *

My Mother died of breast cancer
when I was only eight.
Why when she was very young
was this to be her fate?

She was talented and gifted
in many different ways.
She shared these gifts with many
all of her short days.

Then cancer moved in
and it was a different tale.
Her body became weak
and her organs frail.

She fought the fight,
doing all she could
But the cancer was stronger
and eventually would...

Take her young life and leave me behind
to try and find my own way.
I was young and confused and wondered -
what I should do or say.

There is no answer to the question,
Why, dear Lord, did she die?
She left me alone to raise myself
always asking the question, why?

---

* *"c" is for cancer, written with a small "c."*
I will not acknowledge it with a capital.

One in Three

*One in four was the count.
Now it's one in three.
Why am I surprised to hear
that now, it's also me?*

*Breast cancer has exploded.
and everyone is at risk.
One women in three will get this disease
then be put on a list.*

*The list of survivors - or another statistic
for now a number are you.
A certain percentage will get it again,
regardless of what they do.*

*It is a great mystery of who and why
some people elude this disease.
Those of us not in that group
are very, rarely, at ease.*

Moving On

Choices

"A needle biopsy, surgery, or wait,"
were the choices given to me.
This little lump just sat there
so now we needed to see...

Just what it was - so the choice was made.
Surgery it will be.
There will be no problem, I did think,
but it was a frightening time for me.

"The margins aren't clear, another surgery we'll do."
"It is a malignant growth I did find."
"We must go back in and get it out
and we'll get it all - this time."

How can my Doctor be so loving and kind
when this kind of news she must share.
Very professional but tender, and real.
I'm glad to have a Doctor - who cares.

Moving On

Where Few Go

She came, like a warm breeze, into my life
to encourage and to support me.
Her love for the Lord and a warm, beautiful, smile
was all that I could see.

I was frightened going into surgery number one;
but a steady, loving presence was she.
As we waited for the surgeon to appear
she was a calming influence on me.

I know she was an angel from God
sent when I was in need.
An angel, with skin, to hold my hand
and through this time - to lead.

I'll be eternally grateful to her.
She moved in where few would go.
Thank you, Lord, for this angel with skin -
she was there when I was so low.

Moving On

The Treatments

Moving On

Young and Male

*A young male intern was assigned to me
to monitor how my radiation would go.
He's young - and male - so I asked myself,
"What about breast cancer could he know?"*

*How could I relate to this young man?
Could I share my concerns with him?
I have sons about his same age
and would never confide in them.*

*But looks are very deceiving.
This young man was a treasure to me.
He was bright and informed about his work
and compassionate as he could be.*

*Yes, I've learned from experience.
I can't make judgments so fast.
It's the intangible things on the inside
those are the things that do last.*

Moving On

Blue Dots

My three blue dots I'll not remove.
They are my badge of courage.
I'll wear them all the rest of my life
and will never be discouraged.

For these blue dots did mark the spot
where the radiation could go.
Into my body to kill those cells
so the cells would never grow.

Grow up to be more cancer,
that horrid dreadful word.
But, my blue dots are the guide lines
for that cancer to be deterred.

Many today have blue dots
and if you have them too...
Be proud you wear the 'blue dots'
for it shows what you've been through.

———————

(Before you have radiation,
you are tattooed with blue dots.)

Moving On

High Heels and a White Coat

*I knew she was coming for my exam
for her high heels would click on the floor.
She was businesslike and efficient
but smiled as she entered the door.*

*"Another treatment, I can not do."
"I'm so tired and beat-up today."
"You're here - and you will be treated,"
was all that she did say.*

*At first I thought she was very tough
and had no feelings at all.
As time went on I saw another side
and then understood her call.*

*A strong, positive force she must be
encouraging in what she does say.
But under that clean white coat of hers
lies a broken heart many - a - day.*

Moving On

Radiation

*To go through radiation
is like being buried alive.
I'm locked down in the bowels of the earth
hoping I will survive.*

*I'm put upon a steel table
the technicians call a 'couch,'
Tucked into my special cradle
where I lie and don't say, 'Ouch.'*

*The radiation beams are aligned
with my tattooed blue dots.
"Hold very still," they do say;
"don't move a tittle or jot."*

*Out they go and slam the door
of steel which is six feet wide.
There I am, all alone,
wondering if I have died.*

*The massive machine now warms up
with its very special hum.
The lights go off, then on again,
the machine now sounds like a drum.*

*I count to twenty over and over
then pray all of my prayers.
Is God really in here with me
and does He really care?*

Clones

Everyday for seven weeks
I knew I had to go.
I had to have radiation
if I felt high or low.

It mattered not what my mind did say
as long as my body was there.
I disrobed with all the others
to wait upon my chair.

It's a solemn group of old and young
all dressed just alike.
Hospital gowns that are too short
and on some - too tight.

With a half smile, I look at the others,
but what can I really say?
The prognosis on some is very bleak,
but at least they have - this day.

At last, the nurse calls my name.
"Follow me, it's now your turn."
I get on the steel table and lie very still
for this is what science has learned...

That seven weeks of radiation
can perhaps put at bay -
That cancer which has caused me
many a fear-filled day.

Others

"Don't get involved with the others,"
was the advice given to me.
"When you go for radiation
keep to yourself - so you won't see..."

"The pain and fear in the eyes of others,
as they sit and wait their turn."
Why, dear Lord, this young boy?
What is he suppose to learn?

*He started his treatments seven weeks ago
and looked like a normal teenager.
Now, he's so thin and very weak
it's hard for me to measure...*

*Just how this treatment - everyday -
has benefited him.
He's lost his hair, he can not eat,
he's weak, and tired, and thin.*

*It's hard to look others in the eye
and give my support to them.
It takes energy I don't have
for I'm fighting myself to win...*

*This battle over cancer
that has set me aside for awhile.
To learn the lessons I must learn
- from this most challenging trial.*

Human Touch

*The 'human touch' is a special thing
that can mean so very much.
When you're down or sick or all alone
a touch can help a bunch.*

*During the radiation process
when I'm all alone in the room,
The last thing I remember is
that 'touch' - not all the gloom.*

*That 'human touch' and those little words,
"We will come back to you.
Hold very still for this dose,
don't move whatever you do."*

*Through this challenging experience,
there is one thing that's very clear.
It's that 'human touch' that means so much
when my heart is filled with fear.*

Moving On

The Follow Up

Moving On

A Doctors' Knowledge

*Doctors come
and Doctors go,
But how much do
they really know?*

*About the diseases
attacking man
They're working hard
doing the best they can.*

*But so many things
are unknown still,
Is surgery needed
or only a pill?*

*So don't pin your hopes
on a Doctors' knowledge,
They're just like you,
they've gone to college.*

*For advance study
with degrees and such -
but many questions
remain for this bunch.*

First Checkup

*Fear of the unknown - of hurt and pain -
but without a check up there is no gain.*

*In my head, I know, that this is true
and a checkup now, I must do.*

*But, the memory of what has gone on before...
radiation, the steel room, locked behind the door.*

*When I was in that cold, sterile room
My thoughts would often focus on doom.*

*Will this radiation work? Put the cancer away?
Or just prolong it for another day?*

*Will this keep recurring year after year?
Once I have had it - it's always a fear.*

*Fear that it still lives inside of me;
Regardless of all the things I do flee.*

*Eat right, exercise, this pill for sure.
These things will all help with my cure.*

*To cure the cancer - well, I doubt.
But many women have won this bout.*

Moving On

The Mammogram

The films have been taken.
I sit here and wait.
Wondering, just wondering,
what will be my fate?

What word will the Doctor
give to me?
One more treatment or -
will I be free?

The flip of a coin, a turn
of the screw,
Will effect for the future
just what I will do.

Will it be good news
I hear this day?
Or, "You must come back
for a longer stay."

More examining and testing
we'll run on you,
To see what medically
we must do.

Moving On

*To keep cancer in check
just a while longer,
While medical science
gets much stronger.*

*The doctors are smarter
than those of the past.
Eventually this disease
will not last.*

*None will have cancer
someday soon
But in the present -
I'm locked in this room.*

My Oncologist

*How can she be so up
when dealing with death all day?
Her attitude is incredible -
up beat in what she does say.*

*"It's the human spirit I deal with,
and that's awesome to behold.
The determination to conquer cancer -
is a story that needs to be told."*

*"I've seen many miracles happen
when we had all given up,
but the will and fight of that human spirit
is what daily fills my cup."*

*Perhaps by being so close to death
she appreciates life in a new way.
She knows what's important - and what's not -
that's why she's up beat each day.*

Moving On

I'm All Yours

"Once I'm yours, I'm all yours"
my Doctor said to me.
After my very long wait
to go to her - to see...

Just where this cancer is today
and how my life is going.
Mentally, spiritually, and physically
- just what am I now showing?

Mentally it doesn't own me
as it did awhile ago.
Physically, I feel stronger again
after I'd been so low.

But it's my spiritual life that has saved me.
It has turned me completely around.
With trust and faith in the living Lord
my life is now very sound.

Moving On

Life Goes On

Moving On

A Pretty Face

I saw a pretty face today.
Her smile did captivate me.
As I started talking with her
what she said astonished me.

A beautiful face, charm in her speech,
also a sparkling smile.
This lady, I thought, has it all,
good looks, and such great style.

But we never know what does lie
behind each smiling face.
We only see the outside
and don't understand the pace.

The pace of what one goes through,
and how they have survived.
The fight, the tears, and the great fears,
just to be alive.

Behind that precious, smiling face,
her treatments she just finished.
Radiation, chemo, the fears involved,
but it did not diminish,

The essence of who she is today,
and why she will go far,
Her Spirit and Soul are very strong
they connect her to her Star.

Her Star, her God, her Higher Being,
is what does make her glow.
He's leading, guiding, and holding her close
even when she's so low.

Cocktail Party

I saw him at a cocktail party,
just the other night,
What he said to me
had such great power and might.

My soul was touched deep down inside
when he spoke these words to me,
"I've been praying for you daily, Sue,
and I'm so glad to see,

You up and about and doing well
after such a year,
But you're still in my daily prayers,
and will remain there, my dear."

How very special to have a friend
that lifts me up each day.
To place me in the Lord's hands
as he does pray and pray.

The power and strength from such a gift,
I know in my heart for sure,
God hears my friend, as he goes to prayer,
and speeds along my cure.

Moving On

Victims - No More!

*Cancer that horrible dreadful word
will soon not give such fear;
To the mothers, daughters, and women friends
we love and hold so dear.*

*"Not victims anymore," we'll shout,
"but survivors at long last.
We'll live and love and be mindful always,
but not remain in the past."*

Moving On

Beautiful Smile

I've watched her now for two days
flashing a wonderful smile.
She's charming, upbeat, and happy
so I continue to watch awhile.

She moved through the day playing golf,
and a very good game she can play.
Everyone loves this beautiful lady -
so positive in all she does say.

On the final day of the tournament
to her, I chanced to speak;
And what she said astonished me
- it knocked me off my feet.

"Yes, cancer is my companion.
She is with me every day.
I've learned so much from her
but I wish she would go away!"

What a strong and lovely woman;
she carries this burden so well.
Lord, I lift her up to you,
heal her - and make her well.

Moving On

Waiting in the Wings

*Hats off to those who wait in the wings,
while their loved one goes through cancer.
They are there day after day
wishing they did have an answer...*

*To help, to assist, to calm the fears
of the one they love so much.
But there is nothing that they can do
- so they just show up a bunch.*

*To just be there, to hold their hand,
to listen to them chatter.
Anything, to divert their mind
just what, it does not matter.*

*It's a difficult time for all
and there is nothing you can do.
But you must show up - and be present,
for that's what gets them through.*

*To see your loved one filled with fear
and physically so beat up.
Tears you apart on the inside - but -
it's important that you - show up!*

I've Learned

"How has cancer changed your life?"
she said to me today.
"What have you learned from this experience;
what would you like to say?"

What have I learned, what have I changed,
from this traumatic ordeal?
I have learned many valuable lessons
that now make my life more real.

I've learned to set some boundaries.
I've learned to not always be on the go.
I've learned to choose friends who support me,
and I've learned to just say, "No."

I've learned I have many blessings
and my family is quality.
But the greatest lesson I did learn was
God still loves and cares for me.

This is a publication of :

Blue Dot Publishing
P.O. Box 60725
Palo Alto, CA 94306

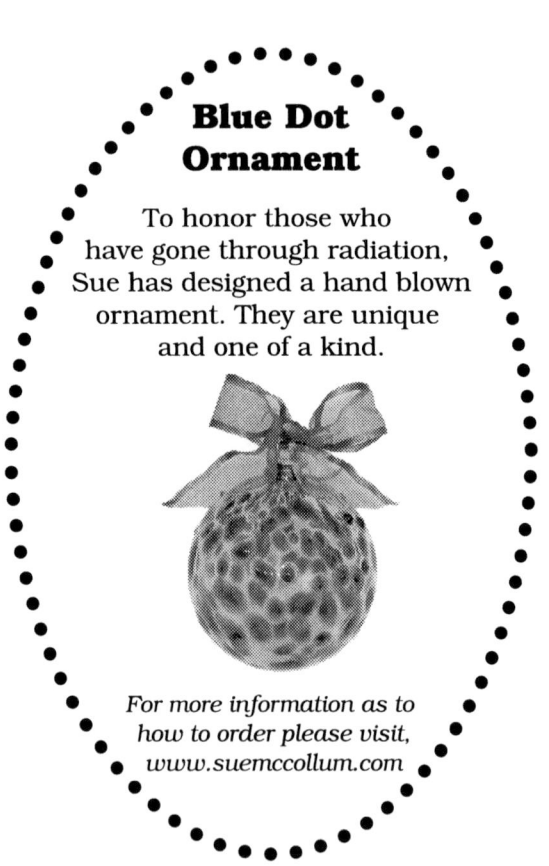

Blue Dot Ornament

To honor those who have gone through radiation, Sue has designed a hand blown ornament. They are unique and one of a kind.

For more information as to how to order please visit, www.suemccollum.com

Proceeds from the sale of this book and ornament will be distributed to cancer research and cancer support groups.

Book and CD Order Form

Name: _____

Address: _____

City:_____ State:_____ Zip:_____

Telephone:_____ e-mail:_____

Book: **Moving On (before and after cancer)**

    Book Quantity _____ at $12.95/each _____

CD: **Moving On (before and after cancer)**

    CD Quantity _____ at $14.95/each _____

Book: **BRAVE and FREE**

    Book Quantity _____ at $14.95/each _____

Book: **Real Love Stories Have No Ending...**

    Book Quantity _____ at $14.95/each _____

Book: **Who Holds the Key?**

    Book Quantity _____ at $14.95/each _____

Shipping and Handling – one to three books $6.00 _____

    Add $.50 per book after that _____

If shipped in California, add CA sales tax of 8.25% _____

    Total: _____

Mail Orders to:
Blue Dot Publishing
P.O. Box 60725
Palo Alto, CA 94306 U.S.A.

Checks only:
Payable to Blue Dot Publishing
Please allow ten days
to process your order

To order on line, please visit: www.suemccollum.com